A book by AND CO & about.me

AND CO

AND CO believes in empowering the future workforce by providing people with the knowledge and technology they need to run their careers as successful businesses.

From proposal to payment: AND CO gives independent workers more time to do what they love—their work.

So, why did we write this book? Beyond our software, we've made it our mission to arm freelancers with an ever-growing list of additional resources to help them grow their businesses to their fullest potential. As the leading support system for freelancers, we've contributed to the broader movement through partnerships with the Freelancers Union, which have helped bring to life policy changes such as the "Freelance Isn't Free Act," and Envato, which offers more than 9 million digital products to freelance creatives and engineers. We even partnered with Death to Stock to provide freelancers with a completely free slate of deck templates to use (and.co/the-deck-stack).

We've written three books designed to help people take their freelance businesses to the next level, maintain a blog that houses regularly updated best practices (and.co/blog); and distribute a weekly Gig List (and.co/gig-list) that's the product of hours of research into the most interesting and exciting freelance gigs posted each week. We even launched a comprehensive study on the state of freelance, called "The Slash Workers" (and.co/slash-workers), which is helping promote the new face of the independent economy and reverse the so-called freelance stigma.

Read more about our mission here: and.co/mission.

ABOUT.ME

about.me helps freelancers, entrepreneurs, and side-hustlers make a name for themselves.

In just a few minutes, you can create a page to present who you are and what you do. With about.me, you can grow your client list or audience, market yourself without the stress, and centralize your work in just one link.

INTRODUCTION

"Growth hacking" is an oft-used term in the startup and tech world with varying definitions. And we are certainly not helping things by including the word "hack" in every chapter title.

So, what does that even mean, hacking? Mark Zuckerberg, who would seem to have an at-least foundational understanding of what it takes to scale a business, has described it as "building something quickly or testing the boundaries of what can be done." Applied to growth initiatives—growing your audience and thereby your business—growth hacking is a new way of approaching strategies to scale a company. Companies with a focus on growth hacking prioritize small, rapid iterations and ongoing testing, and operate under the premise that speed kills and efficiency is king.

Among the more famous examples of a successful growth hacking campaign is Jet.com's Jet Insiders campaign, which allowed early users to invite their friends to climb up a public leaderboard and ultimately, for a few, claim shares of company stock. (Three years after launching, Jet.com sold to Walmart for $3 billion.) Airbnb, today valued at $31 billion, once resorted to gaming Craigslist to post ads for its rental properties. Hey, we all have to start somewhere, right?

Which brings us to you. We wrote this book because we believe that freelancers are more empowered than ever before, and that the very nature of freelance is fundamentally changing from that of short-term, temporary drifts of employment to long-term, independently-run businesses. More than a designer, coder, copywriter—whatever you call yourself—you're an entrepreneur. It's time to start treating your freelance business like just that, a business, and scale your efforts like any business would. Being the enterprising, agile professional you are, growth hacking is just the ticket to get there and we've got just the guide you need to get started.

So, are you ready to grow (and read the word "hack" or a variant of it more than 103 times)?

Hacking Independence

TABLE OF CONTENTS

1. The about.me Hack — 10
2. The Barter Hack — 12
3. The Be Hilarious/Be Human Hack — 14
4. The Before-They-Bounce Hack — 16
5. The Brain Trust Hack — 18
6. The Case Study Hack — 20
7. The Cold Email Hack — 22
8. The Competitive Landscape Hack — 24
9. The DIY Pro Headshot Hack — 26
10. The Dream List Hack — 28
11. The Exclusivity Hack — 30
12. The Faking It Hack — 32
13. The FAQ Page Hack — 34
14. The Get Listed Hack — 36
15. The Guest Blogging Hack — 38
16. The Handwritten Note Hack — 40
17. The HARO Hack — 42
18. The Just-Write-A-Book Hack — 44
19. The Killer Credentials Hack — 46
20. The LinkedIn Headline Hack — 48
21. The LinkedIn Network Hack — 50
22. Make Friends Hack — 52
23. The Name Drop Hack — 54
24. The Newsletter Hack — 56
25. The Oracle Hack — 58
26. The Overachiever Hack — 60

27. The Podcast Hack	62
28. The Product Is King (PIK) Hack	64
29. The Public Information Hack	66
30. The Retargeting Hack	68
31. The Sassy Subject Line Hack	70
32. The SEO Content Hack	72
33. The Social Proof Hack	74
34. The Signature Hack	76
35. The Something for Nothing Hack	78
36. The Strategic Partner Hack	80
37. The User Research Hack	82
38. The VIP Hack	84
39. The Word-of-Mouth Hack	86
40. The Work-Your-Workspace Hack	88

Hacking Independence

HOW TO USE THIS GUIDE

You're busy, so our mission was to compile some of the most replicable, easy-to-implement growth hacks that you can apply today.

To that end, we've focused on concise summaries with actionable steps for getting started. Some of these will make you say, "WOW, I never thought of that!" Others might be more obvious to you, but we've provided the tips you need to take action, instead of revisiting that blog post you've had bookmarked for the past eight months.

We know some of these strategies might prompt questions or further discussion, so we'd love to continue the conversation with you over at hello@andco.nyc or on Twitter twitter.com/andco.

THE ABOUT.ME HACK

Make a name for yourself. This hack will help you create a professional landing page in minutes.

WHAT IS IT?
Looking to land new clients and grow your business? Don't waste time on a website that doesn't yield the results you want. about.me makes it easy to promote your freelance business online. There's no coding, designing, or site maintenance. They handle the hard stuff and you get a simple, yet professional page and personalized domain to centralize your work. Plus, lead generation and appointment scheduling tools, a mini portfolio, and a custom email address to present your business professionally.

HOW DO I DO IT?
Head over to bt.me/aboutmehack to get started for free. Create your free page, and then save up to $100 when you upgrade to their Professional Plan. You'll get to choose a personalized domain with your name in it, a custom email like hello@yourname.me, and unlock access to lead generation and appointment scheduling tools.

WHO CAN I COPY?
Need some inspiration? Check out these pages:

MAX LAPOINTE
Director, Filmmaker, and Traveler in Montreal, Québec, Canada

 Hire me

My name is Max. I am a producer, director and cinematographer from Montreal, Canada. I have shot short & feature films, fashion films, music videos, ad campaigns and documentaries in Montreal, L.A., New York, Bolivia, Spain, Scotland, Mexico and China. Very proud to say my first feature effort as a cinematographer ended up on HotDocs 2014's top ten must sees of the festival and was reviewed as a "startling new documentary", a film with [...] a cinematography reminiscent of Bertolucci, Kieslowski, Haneke and Fellini's films."

Over the last few years, my films and projects were featured on BBC, Discovery Channel, Vogue France, Fucking Young, High Snobiety, TIFF, Fantasia IFFF, HotDocs 2014, NYLA Film Festival, RVCQ 2014, Brooklyn Film Festival and many more.

I'm currently working on the pre-production of my first American feature as cinematographer with an

MEREDITH MOORE CROSBY
Writer, Consultant, and Small Business Owner in Saint Paul, Minnesota

 Sign up for my newsletter

Hi there, I'm Meredith Moore Crosby, a freelance writer living & working in St. Paul, Minnesota. I am currently EVP of Branding at Leverette, Weekes & Company, Inc. as well as a member of Forbes Coaching Council, speaker and lover of funny video clips. In my free time I collect links to smart parenting hacks and management tips for my coaching practice.

I believe in listening to the whole story and brainstorming creative ways for brands to evolve and connect. My past work includes 3M, Comcast, Lincoln Financial, McDonald's Corporation and Verizon.

As a freelancer I am always exploring new opportunities, I would love to talk to you about your next big idea. Drop me a note.

MARILYN RAJU
Interior Decorator, Designer And Stylist in Melbourne, Australia

Book a consultation

Marilyn is passionate about helping clients translate their personality and functional needs into beautiful transitional spaces that tell a story; spaces that are bold, unique and timeless.

With a penchant for pre-loved and vintage furniture and decor, Marilyn loves sourcing items with character for her designs. She aims to introduce layers of texture, pattern and form to create interiors that are visually interesting and dynamic. Her aesthetic is summed up by her design mantra: "Be bold, be brave, be a Maximalist."

Before embarking on her creative journey and entering the world of interior design, Marilyn worked as a management consultant and business specialist helping both large corporations and small businesses. This experience has ensured Marilyn is always committed to providing exceptional service, no matter how large or small a project.

If you want help to create a bold and refined aesthetic for your residential interior or commercial project, please get in touch with Marilyn by clicking on the button above.

EDUCATION
Mercer School of Interior Design
University of Melbourne

Hacking Independence

THE BARTER HACK

Gain complementary business services without spending a dime.

WHAT IS IT?
Bartering is so underrated! As you're building a business, it's easy to watch the expenses pile up or think "I simply can't afford that." Don't forget that your skills are currency in their own right, and they can be used to gain complementary business services. Whether you're a coder, a writer or a designer, chances are there is someone out there who needs your skillset as much as you need theirs.

HOW DO I DO IT?
It's all about identifying the right moments and partners for trading services. Here's a list of situations that may be ripe for bartering:

- Want to attend a conference or event but can't afford the ticket fee? Email the organizers and ask if you can offer your services in exchange for a badge.
- Need help giving your portfolio a facelift? Find a designer or web developer who might be in need of what you bring to the table. If you're a designer/developer, consider all of the talented professionals out there who are need of your services.
- Freelance writers will also have ample opportunities to barter, since basic copywriting is a fairly universal need across most businesses.

Hacking Independence

- Think big! You can even barter your way to upgrades in your personal life. For example, if you're a boutique fitness enthusiast, inquire about consulting in a limited capacity in exchange for free classes.

WHO CAN I COPY?
Here's a somewhat extreme example that's worth a share, if for no other reason than to prove the effectiveness of bartering in general. A few years back, a 12-year-old from Ohio successfully turned a used Playstation gaming console, sold for $40 on Craigslist, into a Chevy Camaro—simply by continually trading up from item to item.

While the purpose of your bartering is generally to receive a complimentary service, of equal value, in exchange for your own services, let Rachel be an inspiration for us all. When it comes to bartering, there's no harm in asking. Have a goal and give it a shot.

Madison teen trades up, turning PlayStation 2 into Camaro with Craigslist

13

THE BE HILARIOUS/BE HUMAN HACK

Humans dig humans. You can be a professional while still showing your humanity.

WHAT IS IT?
As an independent business owner, being buttoned up, professional, on time, etc. is critically important. Your reputation is intrinsically tied to the reputation of your business, so you can't be a hot mess! There's a balance, however. With social media has come a humanization in most industries, and nowadays, having a personality can actually be a competitive advantage.

HOW DO I DO IT?
This one's easy. Just be yourself, but maybe just the PG-13 version. Don't be afraid to crack a joke or two, but make sure it's in the right moment. Have that beer with a client, but make sure your deliverables are handed in well in advance. Impress clients and prospects with your professionalism and work ethic, and then let them see the real you.

WHO CAN I COPY?
Check out this Medium post from Darren Wong, a brand strategist turned solopreneur. You might know him as the creator of the Raindrop Cake, the Instagrammable food sensation has taken New York and LA by storm.

The short post effectively showcases Darren's personality while still establishing credibility. Sure, he uses a few curse words here and there. But all in all, it's well-articulated and his point is well-taken. It's clever and smart, but most importantly, it's also undeniably Darren. You can approach your own content and marketing in a similar fashion.

Darren Wong Follow
Jul 13 · 2 min read

Here's My Shitty Article

A year ago I quit my well paying, comfortable job to create my own company. I founded Raindrop Cake® sparking an international food trend; I had no idea what I was doing. Despite that, I still managed to find some success and has afforded the entrepreneurial lifestyle I've always wanted.

Far be it for me to offer advice, because I still have a lot to learn. What I want to do is share what finally got me over the hump in hopes that it will help other people get over the same hump from idea to execution; so you can eventually quit your 9–5 job too.

Make a shitty thing.

THE BEFORE-THEY-BOUNCE HACK

Capture website visitors before they leave by offering them something new.

WHAT IS IT?
A "bounce" is when a visitor to your blog or website is about to leave the page. Did you know that there are ways to engage visitors even as they are about to go? Enter the Before-They-Bounce Hack. By leveraging a tool like Bounce Exchange (bouncex.com), you can keep people on-site for a bit longer.

HOW DO I DO IT?
There are several tools that are designed to help keep people on-site and increase the odds they convert, the aforementioned Bounce Exchange being one of many. Each of these tools work in a similar capacity, helping you put forth a new offer or piece of content to get visitors to convert before they leave. If you manage a website with significant traffic, then these tools might be a worthwhile investment for you.

WHO CAN I COPY?
Here are a few examples of exit overlays that seek to convert at the moment before a visitor bounces.

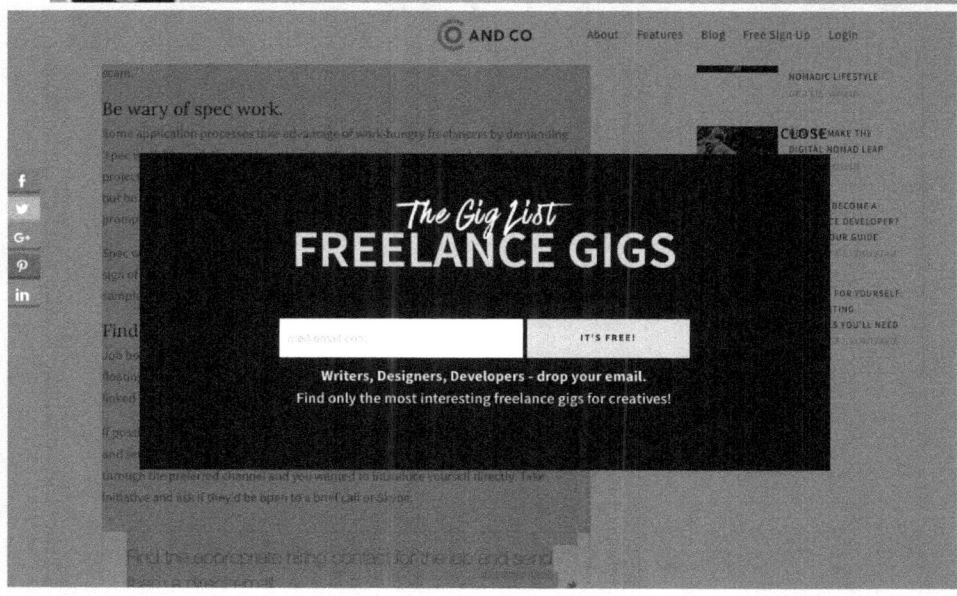

Hacking Independence

THE BRAIN TRUST HACK

Bring people into your business process.

WHAT IS IT?
The "brain trust" was a term made famous by U.S. President Franklin D. Roosevelt during his administration. He used this term to affectionately describe his inner circle: a close group of friends, advisors, experts and confidants who helped guide his decision-making process while in office. As an independent business owner, it's wise to build your own brain trust as it will have two main benefits. The first is that having a brain trust means that you'll have access to people with complementary talents and perspectives to your own, which will only enhance the decisions you make. The second benefit is that keeping a close group of influencers close to your business will ensure these folks are more likely to turn to you for work or refer you to their own networks.

HOW TO DO IT?
The best advice here is to not OVERDO it. Having a brain trust is a great way to capture important feedback, but outreach to and consulting from these individuals should be used sparingly and in critical moments only. Some examples of times where it might make sense to hit up your inner circle:

- You want to change your business tagline, but are torn between two or three contenders.

- You have a draft byline near completion and want to ask your close network a few pointed questions about your POV.
- You have a very mission critical prospect meeting on deck, and you want advice on what will resonate with a specific individual, job title or industry.

WHO CAN I COPY?

You won't find public examples of this, because the key to reaching out to your inner circle is to make it personal, direct and one-to-one. Mass emails and social media posts will be less effective in this regard, since they will lose the feeling of intimacy and exclusivity that a direct email or phone call will provide. Our biggest piece of advice? Keep it short and simple.

Dear [NAME],

I am reaching out to you because I consider you a close friend/ mentor and someone with relevant expertise in [TOPIC]. I am seeking feedback on [WHATEVER YOU WANT FEEDBACK ON HERE] and would be curious to hear your thoughts on it. Of course, I understand you're exceptionally busy, so any high level thoughts here would be much appreciated. If easier, perhaps we can schedule a five to ten minute phone call, if your schedule allows.

Thank you,
[YOUR NAME]

THE CASE STUDY HACK

Paint prospects a clear picture of what you can do for them. Just answer three questions.

WHAT IS IT?
Anyone who's worked in advertising knows how important case studies are. For one, they are the only means by which creative directors can prove their worth, because we all know that "business impact" means little in the agency world. From a marketing/PR standpoint, case studies are an invaluable way to show prospective clients what you're capable of. And because they take the form of short stories, they're often more memorable than stats or a list of capabilities.

HOW DO I DO IT?
Crafting case studies is an art form of sorts, and major advertising agencies hire people, and even teams of people, to focus solely on case studies for award submissions. Here's a secret though: it's not rocket science. Just answer these questions and you'll be on your way to writing a compelling case study for your work:

- **Challenge:** The challenge sets up the entire story. Why is it that the client hired you in the first place? Once you've answered that, disregard it. Yep. Now, think bigger. Beyond the immediate need for hiring you, what is the bigger picture need of the business? Yes, we're telling you to imply credit for solving a problem that was perhaps bigger than what was in the brief, and that's AOK.
  - *Wrong:* "Ford Motors needed a landing page to drive a new promotion."

- *Right:* "Ford Motors, a brand known for its heritage and history, needed a fresh visual direction to promote their biggest sweepstakes of the year among a new audience of millennial car shoppers."
- **Solution:** Here's where you succinctly state what it is you did. Again, think bigger. What unique approach did you take? Was there a particularly creative insight or approach you employed? Did you use data? Use the solution to spell out what makes you awesome at your job (and worthy of work from prospects down the road!).
- **Results:** This section can be tough depending on your line of work, but nothing is impossible. C'mon! You're a freelancer. You make miracles happen on the daily. The most important thing to remember about the results is that it should ladder back to the challenge. Makes sense, right? Client pays you to solve a problem → you actually solve said problem. Data is extremely powerful here, and more important than data is contextualized data. If you're a PR specialist, saying "garnered 100 million earned impressions" is less powerful than saying "increased media mentions by 300%" or "generated $5 million in total media value."

WHO CAN I COPY?

Need inspiration? Browse the "work" sections of any major advertising agency. If you're going to steal, steal from the best.

Hacking Independence

THE COLD EMAIL HACK

Go straight to the source in a few simple steps.

WHAT IS IT?
If you're actively looking for freelance gigs, chances are you're starting with the job boards. Whether it's Indeed, LinkedIn, Dribbble or AND CO's curated Gig List newsletter (sign up: and.co/gig-list), you'll probably be asked to submit your portfolio or resume via a webform. While this helps HR teams manage the influx of applications coming their way, it's not the best way to get in front of a hiring manager. Hack it by employing a few quick steps to get to an actual person.

HOW DO I DO IT?
If you're on the job form page, start with a simple LinkedIn search for the appropriate title and company. For example, if it's a marketing designer role at Foursquare, you might look up their Director of Marketing or CMO. Next, Google the email convention for that company. You can start by searching "@[company].com" (or whatever top-level domain the company uses) and seeing if any personal emails come up. Once you know the convention, it's easy to guess the contact's address. You can even make sure it works before you send with a tool like email-checker.net or Hunter.io (hunter.io).

WHO CAN I COPY?
It helps to have a ready-made template for this type of outreach. Here's a good place to start:

Subject: Candidate for [Role] at [Company]

Hello, [Name],

I saw the posting for [Role] on [Job board] and wanted to reach out directly to express my interest. I am a [personal headline - e.g. "independent UX designer"] with [X] years of relevant experience working with brands like [company A], [company B] & [company C]. I would love to connect this week to discuss the opportunity.

Do you have any availability [provide a few dates/times here]?

Some additional materials if they help:
[Portfolio link]
[LinkedIn URL]
[Other materials as needed]

Best,
[Your name]

THE COMPETITIVE LANDSCAPE HACK

Keep close tabs on your competitive set.

WHAT IS IT?
You might be a business of one, but rest assured, there are likely many other professionals on the market selling a similar product as your own. Keeping tabs on your competitors should be a regular exercise as you scale your business.

HOW DO I DO IT?
Set up a spreadsheet where you plan to actively track individuals or companies in your competitive set. You might include companies that fully align with your offering, as well as those that offer just some of the same types of capabilities. Need help finding competitors? Here are some places to start:

- Google search relevant keywords
- Service databases or portfolio sites
- "Best of" or "top companies" lists and awards in your category
- Press quotes, mentions or guest articles
- Guest speakers at relevant industry events

Hacking Independence

WHO CAN I COPY?

Utilizing a simple SWOT analysis template will help you make your competitive tracking actionable in a way that will strengthen your business. Fill out the below at least once per quarter.

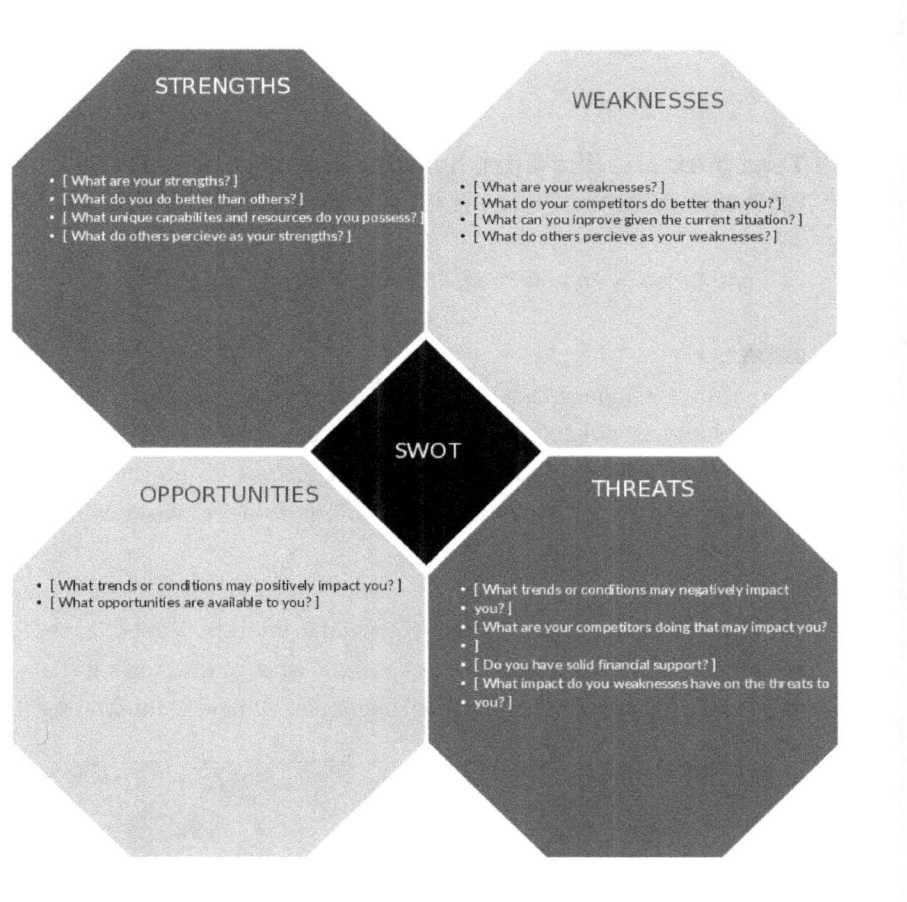

25

Hacking Independence

THE DIY PRO HEADSHOT HACK

Take portraits like a pro by using a poster board as a reflector to amplify natural light and reduce shadows.

Contributed by Andrew Yang, CEO, 500px (about.500px.com).

WHAT IS IT?
A great professional headshot can go far, but who wants to drop several hundred dollars on a photo shoot? Any photographer will tell you that lighting is the foundation of a great portrait. Natural light, like sunshine, is arguably one of the most flattering, easiest types of light to work with—and best of all, it's free.

To get the most out of natural light you need to know how to enhance, aim, and amplify it by using a reflector. At its core, a reflector is just a reflective surface that is used to boost light and eliminate unflattering

Left: Without reflector, Right: With reflector

shadows. Reflectors come in many colors—gold, silver, white—and sizes, but any reflective surface like a white poster board will do.

HOW DO I DO IT?
You'll want to find a location that is not directly in the sun, like the shady side of a building, a room with a window, or somewhere with an overhang. My favorite time to shoot is in the late afternoon when the sun is lower in the sky and the light is not as harsh.

Next, you'll need someone to hold the poster board as close to your subject as possible without being in the frame. You can also ask your subject to hold the reflector like a sunbathing panel, but make sure it's not visible in the shot. Aim the reflector so it's absorbing the sunlight and bouncing onto your subject. Move the reflector around your subject (below, left, right) and watch as the light increases.

You'll know you've found the sweet spot when you see your subject getting brighter and the appearance of shadows are reduced. To an inexperienced eye, it may seem like a subtle shift in brightness, but it becomes very apparent when you take a photo.

Try placing the reflector below, to the left or right side of your subject.

WHO CAN I COPY?
Almost every ad/editorial campaign photographed outdoors uses some kind of reflector to amplify light. Take a closer look at photos to get a better understanding of the quality and direction of natural light.

THE DREAM LIST HACK

Dream big! Keeping a wish list of prospects will keep you on target.

WHAT IS IT?
Managing the day-to-day workload of a freelance business is a full-time job and then some. It can be easy to get buried in the weeds of billable (and nonbillable) work and forget to look ahead toward your North Star. One easy way to keep your eye on the prize is to keep an actively managed spreadsheet or database of "dream clients." See a company doing cool work in a trade publication? Spot a friend who moved to an interesting new startup? Write these down and schedule 30 minutes a month to review your list. Remember, running yourself like a business means proactively going after aspirational clients versus taking on work just to keep the lights on.

HOW DO I DO IT?
Using your preferred project management tool (or perhaps a simple spreadsheet is easiest) to write down companies and individuals with which you'd like to work. Add columns for company name, target (person at company who is most relevant to your business), website URL and contact address. Finally, add a column for why they caught your eye, or where you could see yourself partnering in the future.

WHO CAN I COPY?
A simple spreadsheet will be sufficient for most independent workers, but the method you ultimately choose can be tailored to your liking.

Hacking Independence

The key is having an established place (or app) where all of your leads are captured and well-organized. Always include a status and next steps column so you can keep things moving forward.

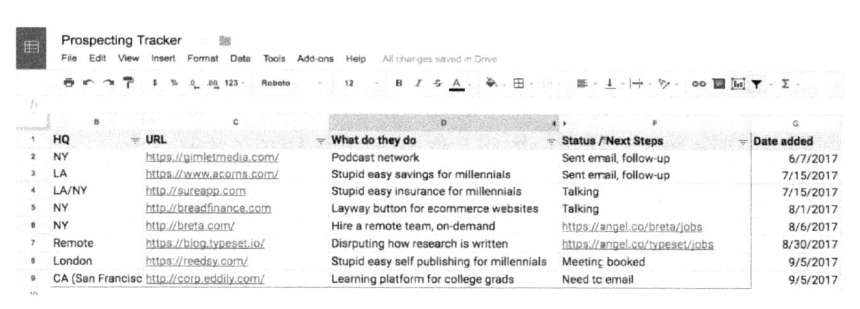

Hacking Independence

THE EXCLUSIVITY HACK

Promote your availability while exuding an air of *unavailability*.

WHAT IS IT?
When you're starting a business, perception is reality—which is why it pays to spend some time honing your personal brand and marketing strategy. One lesson adopted by some of the world's most successful business is to leverage the power of "no." People want what they can't have, and oftentimes exuding an air of unavailability can work in your favor.

HOW TO DO IT?
As you build your business, build a mini-checklist of the boxes you want to tick off before saying "yes" to a potential partner. Use this to a) guide the choices you make with respect to clients, but also b) how you explain your approach to prospects. Merely articulating that you employ such a framework will communicate to prospects that you don't just work with anyone at all. Another pro-tip: Even if you're seeking new partners, avoid coming off as overly eager. Be available, but only to the extent that you can "shift some projects around."

WHO CAN I COPY?
Need help with your checklist? Here are some thought-starters:

- Smart, respectable and trustworthy leadership team
- Product or customer-obsessed culture
- Strategic role despite contract status
- Disrupting [X] sector
- Opportunity for recurring work or a longer-term engagement

LOOKING FOR WORK?
Steal and customize this copy for your LinkedIn status:

> "After several months of back-to-back engagements, I am finally coming up on some limited bandwidth for the next [X] weeks and am looking to take on one additional client. Given my passion for technology, I am looking for mission-driven companies who are seeking contract-based design work to take their branding to the next level. Please email me if you know of anyone."

Hacking Independence

THE FAKING IT HACK

Big companies fake stuff all the time. Here's why you should, too.

WHAT IS IT?
What's the first thing a company does when they pivot, rebrand or launch a new product? They say exactly what it is they are trying to be, before they've ever proven it! It might seem weird to apply this same model to you (your own business), but get used to it. Faking it is the simplest way to become the business you always wanted to be. Some examples:

- Any startup that declares its "disrupting" something or some industry. Newsflash: They probably aren't—at least not yet.
- A tech platform that claims it's the "leading" provider in the space. It's probably not, but they sure as hell want to be.
- A company that completely changes its tagline in an effort to alter perception (e.g. Swarm changing its tagline to "Remember everywhere" to match a product pivot).

HOW TO DO IT?
Pretend you're at a party. You step away from your friends to grab a drink, and a stranger joins the group. You're still in earshot and you can listen in on their conversation. In a perfect world, with your business exactly where you want it to be, how do you want your friends to describe who you are and what you do for work? Jot down a few versions of this and finesse the wording. Some examples:

- Gloria is a UX designer who works with some of the biggest brands in the world. She takes a data-driven approach to her projects, grounding creativity in keen insight into user behavior and design trends.
- Michael is an engineer who partners with rapidly-scaling startups. He specializes in consumer apps, and is known for his ability to deliver on tight deadlines.
- Taylor is a PR strategist who partners with early stage direct-to-consumer product companies. Her clients have appeared in the *New York Times*, *TechCrunch*, *Forbes*, and countless other top-tier publications.

Keep in mind: You can be as aspirational as you like when it comes to how you describe yourself, but be accurate. For example, Michael might not be partnering exclusively with startups yet, but maybe he wants to. For him, it makes sense to isolate this in his description. In the case of Taylor, she probably wants to make sure she actually got those press placements before shouting them from the rooftops.

WHO CAN I COPY?

Need some help overcoming your imposter syndrome? Consider a comprehensive analysis (ncbi.nlm.nih.gov/pubmed/12002965) of more than 130 studies and 23,000 employees, which found that people who demonstrated as high self-monitors (those who frequently adjust their actions based on social cues) were significantly more likely to be promoted into leadership positions. As Wharton professor Adam Grant put it in a recent *New York Times* op-ed:

> *"High self-monitors were more likely than their authentic peers to experiment with different leadership styles. They watched senior leaders in the organization, borrowed their language and action, and practiced them until these became second nature. They were not authentic, but they were sincere. It made them more effective."*

THE FAQ PAGE HACK

Save time with a one-stop shop for common client questions.

WHAT IS IT?
As a freelancer, you know that time is money. The less time you spend on non-billable work, the more time you have freed up to take on paying projects. It's that simple. One easy way to cut down on the back-and-forth, and augment your marketing, is to build a FAQ page into your portfolio or personal website. There, take the time to list out common questions you get asked about your services. Answer them in a complete, yet human, way to showcase your personality. The next time a prospective client asks you a question: BOOM. Send them the link. It'll save you time and make you look more legit.

HOW DO I DO IT?
Start with a simple document and a five minute brainstorm session. In no particular order, jot down the questions you commonly field. Next, allot another five minutes to think about questions that might serve to help you in a marketing capacity, e.g. "Which creative awards have you won?" or "Who else have you worked with?" Once you've done this, review the list in aggregate, removing any potentially sensitive questions (such as questions regarding pricing and rates). Finally, open a Google doc and answer the questions as you would in conversation. Keep responses no longer than two sentences.

WHO'S DOING IT WELL?
Check out these FAQ pages for inspiration:

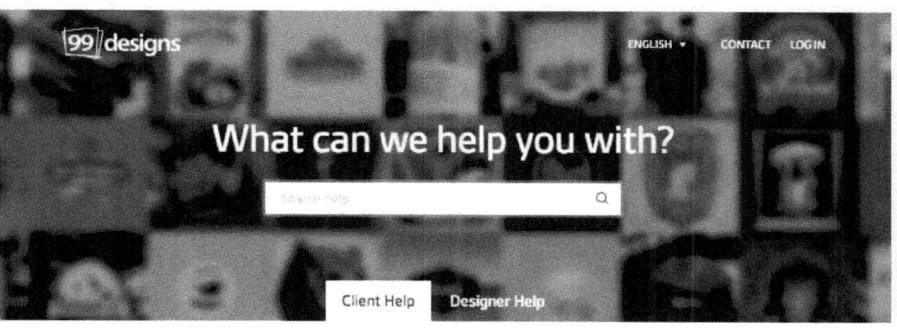

The Basics
Just signed up and have questions? Look no further!

Uploading & Transcoding
Questions about uploading & transcoding can be found here.

101s
This is where you can read extensive articles that explain the ins and outs of SoundCloud.

Community
Here are some questions and answers about following, unfollowing, meetups and more.

Account Access
What to do when you've lost access to your account.

Embedded Players / Widgets
Embed sounds on the web with our range of widgets.

Tracks & Playlists
Learn more about creating and managing sounds and sets.

Mobile & Apps
Frequently asked questions related to our mobile site and apps.

99 Designs: Simple & well-organized

Soundcloud: Visually appealing iconography

Cards Against Humanity: Human and on-brand

Hacking Independence

THE GET LISTED HACK

Submit yourself to relevant directories to get discovered.

WHAT IS IT?
Submitting yourself to lists and databases might seem like an arcane activity in the digital age, but it works. Clients trust directories to help narrow their searches, and by getting yourself included in these lists, you'll increase your discoverability.

HOW DO I DO IT?
Let's start with the obvious ones. Depending on your business, this could be Yelp, Angie's List, Google's Business Directory, or a handful of others you can see by finding competitors to these sites on websites like Spyfu. But that's not where it ends. There are hundreds, if not thousands of other directories that are more local and regional that get trafficked and can produce new customers for you. Have an agency in Los Angeles? Submit to http://agencylist.org/la. By searching your business type and the area you're located, it's likely you'll find directories on first page results of a Google Search. Find those directories and get listed!

WHO CAN I COPY?
Everyone! Everyone is listed in directory upon directory nowadays, but it can be very clear on who to copy. Wherever you're being listed, take a look at a few of the other listings. How are they rated? What

are they doing correctly to make sure that their public profile shines among the rest? Find a bunch of examples that you love, learn from them, and get to building your own profile that will shine among the rest!

THE GUEST BLOGGING HACK

Increase your digital footprint and improve SEO by contributing to blogs.

WHAT IS IT?
Guest blogging involves submitting content pieces to established blogs and publications in your area of expertise. A form of bartering, you provide thought leadership on a topic which relates to your business, and then publication gains fresh content to keep their audience engaged. In one famous case, Buffer co-founder Leo Widrich said that the company used guest-blogging to grow Buffer's audience from 0 to 100,000. In nine months, they wrote 150 guest posts (nearly one every business day).

HOW DO I DO IT?
Start with a list of popular publications and blogs that cover topics relevant to your area of expertise. This list might include personal blogs, if the audience size warrants it, and if the individuals are non-competitive. When you reach out, have a high-level pitch in mind so they can quickly assess the topic and your credibility to write about it. When you submit the article, be sure to include any UTM (tracking) codes you want to use to assess performance, and optimize the content around a target keyword for which you'd like to rank (e.g. "UX design best practices" or "copywriting tips for startups.")

WHO CAN I COPY?

When it comes to guest posting, nobody does it better than Buffer. Here's a sample pitch Widrich shared with *Search Engine Journal*:

> Hi guys,
>
> As a guy just starting out with a few basic webdesign lessons, I found onextrapixel extremely helpful, so just a quick thank you on that note.
>
> I wanted to ask if you are interested in a guestpost that I have drafted, which I titled "10 Tools To Make The Most of Twitter". It covers a few of the latest Twitter Tools, which help me a lot to stay productive.
>
> I hope you can let me know if you think the post could be interesting for you.
>
> For reference of my writing style, I published recently on:*Six Revisions* *SocialMediaExaminer* *Inspiredm*
>
> Best,
> Leo

Hacking Independence

THE HANDWRITTEN NOTE HACK

Take five minutes to infuse a personal touch in your communications.

WHAT IS IT?
Back in the day—before we had Slack, email, fax machines and the like—people wrote notes. Handwritten ones. And they were awesome. The thing about handwritten notes is that they are easy (takes five minutes), cheap (stamps cost $.50) and go a long when when it comes to cutting through the noise. Want to say thanks to a client for their partnership? Send a note. Having trouble getting a response from a prospect. Send a note.

HOW DO I DO IT?
Since you're a business, we recommend investing some money into simple note cards or letterhead. Moo.com is a great option for that! From there, it's pretty easy. Just write, send and watch the results pour in.

WHO CAN I COPY?
Not to toot our own horn, but we've been sending personal notes to every new AND CO member for quite some time now. We love connecting with our community on a more personal level, and who doesn't love getting mail?

Candace Nicholson
@Incandescere

Like the personal touch of a handwritten Thank You note, @andco. Well played. 👏 Well played, indeed.

Hacking Independence

THE HARO HACK

Get your business in the news without hiring a publicist.

WHAT IS IT?
Help A Reporter Out (helpareporter.com) is a service that pairs journalists with credible sources across a range of industries, including business, tech, travel, and PR. The model is so simple, it's genius: reporters submit story ideas they are in need of sources for, and HARO's editors vet them and compile them into a newsletter that's distributed multiple times a day. If you're a business owner, you can sign up to receive the free newsletter. The newsletter provides contact emails for each story, so when you see something relevant to you, you can pitch to the reporter directly.

HOW DO I DO IT?
You can sign up for a free HARO account. You'll start receiving emails instantly. New to pitching journalists? It's not rocket science. Here's a simple outline to follow when pitching reporters:

- **Subject:** Make it compelling and relevant to their article (e.g. "Graphic designer with opinion on website design trends")
- **Email:** Make it short and sweet. Succinctly describe who you are, and why you're qualified to weigh in. Make it easy for the journalist to quote you by providing a single quote or bulleted quotes that they can easily copy and paste should they opt out of a more formal interview.

- **Sign off:** It's always good to end with a question to keep the conversation going. This can be an inquiry around their ability to chat via the phone, or a general question about their story (see below example).

WHO DO I COPY?

Here's an example:

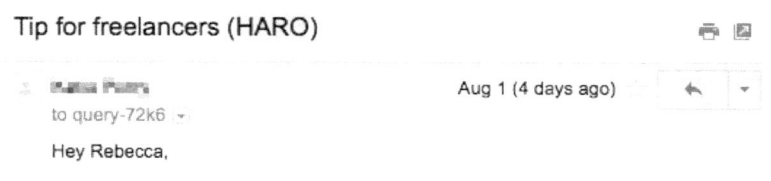

THE JUST-WRITE-A-BOOK HACK

Promoting your expertise and attracting new customers is as simple as putting pen to paper.

WHAT IS IT?
When you think of what goes into writing a book, you might consider how the great literary minds of the past and present have toiled for months, even years, to perfect their masterpieces. That's one type of writing: writing as art. In the business world, however, writing can serve a much more practical purpose. It can educate, inform and generate credibility as you scale your business. The good news is that while you'll need to be a competent writer, nobody is expecting Hemingway-esque prose. They simply want to learn something new.

HOW DO I DO IT?
The first step is to ask yourself if you have any business writing a book. If you're an ambitious solopreneur, you'll no doubt know your sweet spot. What is a topic for which you have credibility through experience or general knowledge? Start with an outline an enlist the help of a copyeditor to help bring your ideas to life. Don't have the dough to hire an editor? No problem. Diligent proofing and apps like Hemmingway (hemingwayapp.com) and Grammarly (grammarly.com) will help here.

One area where you won't want to be stingy is design: Make sure that your pages are laid out in a clean fashion, even if the design is

Hacking Independence

barebones. In terms of distribution, we recommend creating a landing page that can be used to capture emails in exchange for a digital version of a book. Services like Pay With A Tweet (paywithatweet.com) can also be helpful in promoting social shares.

WHO CAN I COPY?
AND CO has published three books thus far (including this one!). Our first two, "Welcome to Your Independence" (and.co/how-to-freelance) and "ANYWHERE: The Essential Handbook for Digital Nomads, By Digital Nomads" (and.co/digital-nomad-book) have garnered a combined 20,000 downloads to date with no paid media support.

Freelance copywriter Annie Maguire is proof-positive that you don't have to be a startup like us to do it. She published her own book of tips for going independent titled, "From Fulltime to Freelance," and hosts it for purchase on her personal website (anniemaguire.com). Visitors can download the first chapter for free.

Hacking Independence

THE KILLER CREDENTIALS HACK

Get your creds deck on point and watch your freelance biz flourish.

WHAT IS IT?
A creds deck is a PPT, Keynote or PDF document that clearly articulates what your business is capable of doing, and demonstrates your ability to deliver on those capabilities, in the eyes of a new potential partner. A staple in the agency world, crafting a killer creds deck is a helpful way to share your background and skillset each time you meet a new prospect. And the best part? If you do it right the first time, your level of effort moving forward will be minimal.

HOW DO I DO IT?
The best creds decks are ten slides or less. They should serve the purpose of introducing yourself/your business, as well as your capabilities, all while establishing credibility via social proof, which might include partner logos, testimonials, case studies and press coverage. If you don't have design skills, utilize a template or enlist a designer friend to help you get the deck ready for primetime. Here's a simple outline to follow:

- **Cover slide:** Company name and tagline
- **Slide 1:** Vision and value prop: Why do you exist? What is the underlying theme spanning across all of your projects and clients? Think big!

- **Slide 2:** Articulate the primary challenge your services aim to solve.
- **Slide 3:** Approach/solution – How do you do it?
- **Slide 4:** Specific skills or credentials, e.g. a list of things you sell.
- **Slide 5:** Who have you worked with before / who are you working with currently? Use logos.
- **Slide 6:** Short case studies (1 to 3 max)
- **Slide 7:** Thought-starters specific to the client you're presenting to.
- **Slide 8:** Team slide: Who will be helping you with this project? Will any collaborators or support players be involved? If yes, include them here.
- **Slide 9:** Pricing / Rates. Note: Some freelancers prefer to leave this out and reserve numbers talk for an in-person conversation.
- **Slide 10:** Recap contact info.

WHO CAN I COPY?
Slideshare houses many creds decks that can be used for inspiration. If you're looking for the crème de la crème in terms of design, check out any agency creds deck.

THE LINKEDIN HEADLINE HACK

Succinctly state your business in the headline.

Contributed by Max Pete, Digital Marketing & Website Design Consultant (maxpete.co)

WHAT IS IT?
Linkedin is one of the best networking tools available to anyone in the workforce. For freelancers and independent workers, being active on Linkedin can mean the difference between having a full client list to an empty one. However, many freelancers and independent workers aren't using Linkedin to their advantage.

One easy hack that helps pull your name up in search results and immediately helps describe what you do to a potential client is changing your "Headline" to reflect your skill set and experience level. For example, you might be a digital marketing and content creation genius, so you will want to make sure your headline reflects that. It would look something like "Content Marketing Strategist | Digital Marketing Professional with over [X] years of experience."

HOW DO I DO IT?
Go into your Linkedin profile today, and click on edit headline. If your headline isn't already reflecting of your skill set, not just your job, change it today.

Hacking Independence

WHO CAN I COPY?
Check out Brian Honigman or Chris Do.

Hacking Independence

THE LINKEDIN NETWORK HACK

Work your network to grow your business.

Contributed by Dennis Williams, LinkedIn Top Voice, Content Strategist & Speaker (linkedin.com/in/denniswilliamsii)

WHAT IS IT?
Engaging in conversation with those who comment on or share your content is crucial for growing your readership on any platform, but it's ten times more important for your success on LinkedIn.

The LinkedIn algorithm can be used to reach a large number of people via a network effect. When a user likes or comments on an article of yours, it appears on his/her personal feed. Thus, it's important to start a conversation with those who have engaged with your work.

Getting in front of the masses isn't by chance, and thankfully, the hack that follows can help gain exposure and quality conversations as a LinkedIn user.

HOW DO I DO IT?
LinkedIn posts are an excellent way to have others in your network help amplify your thought leadership. To get started, tag two or three individuals who could add to your conversation in the first comment on your own LinkedIn post. Don't be afraid to mention other thought leaders to showcase other interesting perspectives. Each week, make a point to track how it impacts your audience growth. The platform's

algorithm rewards ongoing conversation, ultimately bringing third and fourth-degree audiences to what you've written.

Choose a few influencers or active members of your network and keep them in mind whenever you publish content in the future. Not everyone will have an interest or passion in your content, so it's important to understand how they could add insight to the conversation. After you've done this prior research, try it out with a couple of members you've established a relationship with and tag them in your next LinkedIn post to help grow a larger dialogue.

WHO CAN I COPY?

Need inspiration? Mimic two professionals who are doing it right:

- Michael Spencer: linkedin.com/in/michaelkspencer
- Josh Fechter: linkedin.com/in/joshuafechter

Hacking Independence

MAKE FRIENDS HACK

Because freelancers refer work to other freelancers.

Contributed by Kaleigh Moore, freelance writer (kaleighmoore.com).

WHAT IS IT?
Data from Freelancers Union shows that 81 percent of freelancers refer work to one another. For this reason, creating a network of freelance friends an important business development exercise for any aspiring solopreneur. With a network of professionals that do similar work, you have people to can turn to during slow times to see if they have any overflow work they need help with. On the same hand, during weeks when you're too busy, you can return the favor and refer out some of the jobs you just can't take on at the moment. It's a win-win!

HOW DO I DO IT?
Here are some simple ways to get started:

- Participate in relevant online and IRL communities (e.g. Facebook groups, forums, Slack channels, and Freelancers Union) and be deliberate about making friends in your freelance niche.
- Set up virtual coffee dates via Skype each month with new freelancers you want to get to know better.
- When gigs come your way that are out of scope of not a fit, refer them to fellow freelancers. Good karma comes back around!

WHO CAN I COPY?

Freelance writer Emma Siemasko says that 50 to 80 percent of her work comes via referrals from fellow freelancers. She recommends regularly checking in with your freelance network and remembering to be a returner of referrals so that these relationships don't become too one-sided.

Hacking Independence

THE NAME DROP HACK

So simple, so effective.

WHAT IS IT?
We know, we know. We hate namedroppers, too. But there's a reason people spew out the names of all of rich/powerful/well-connected/intelligent/influential/you-name-it people they know. Because it works.

HOW DO I DO IT?
Chances are, you don't have a photographic memory making it difficult to recall all of the people you know on command. For this reason, it's helpful to maintain a simple spreadsheet of key contacts, or at the very least stay on top of your LinkedIn activity.

WHO DO I COPY?
How's this for a stretch goal? Steven Burda, a master-connector, has the most connections on LinkedIn. While that's impressive in and of itself, he also boasts 2,000+ recommendations, which serve as built-in "name drops" on this profile.

Steven Burda, MBA · 2nd

Senior Financial & Business Professional. Strategic Thinker. Entrepreneur. Mover & Shaker. Most Connected on Linkedin!

BridgInform Technologies, LLC • University (Doctorate Degree Program)

Recommendations

Received (2,215)   Given (10)

Tammy Bowers
CEO - Inspiring Hearts LLC – Tender Loving AdvoCare –Hand in Hand with You & Your Loved Ones! (Private Patient Advocate)

March 2, 2016, Tammy worked with Steven but at different companies

I have known Steve for quite some time, appreciating his business model mostly due to the fact that we mirror the same values and appreciate building those business relationships. Steve is a man of his word, eager to help others, with integrity and sincerity. this goes along way in my book and its refreshing as we enjoy connecting to those individuals who emulating those same qualities. Thank you Steve for setting the bar as a game changers in the industry, we value you and thank you for all you do!!

Hutch Hutcherson
10,000+ ♦ M.Ed. ♦ VP Graduation Alliance ♦ K-12 EdTech ♦ Dropouts ♦ At-Risk ♦ Assessment ♦ Intervention ♦ Job Skills

September 12, 2015, Hutch worked with Steven but at different companies

Steven Burda is an amazing professional, a dedicated father, a Fortune 500 super-star Consultant, and a financial guru. On top of all of that, he is the most connected person in the world on LinkedIn. I absolutely love what Steven is doing with BurdEye. I believe that Steven epitomizes the evolution that is occurring in the way that people do business in the world. Steven's skill at using his own work ethic backed by technology and leveraged by

One area where Burda can improve? Despite receiving 2,215 recommendations, he has only given out ten. Share the wealth! Via linkedin.com/in/burda

THE NEWSLETTER HACK

Curate a regular newsletter as a value add to current and potential customers.

WHAT IS IT?
We all know how hard it is to earn attention in a crowded inbox, so proceed with caution. If content isn't your bread and butter, skip this hack. But if you're investing in developing articles and other forms of thought leadership, or if you have a unique perspective that ties to your business offering, then you might consider creating a regular newsletter and promoting it to entice subscriber sign-ups.

HOW DO I DO IT?
Before you dive into MailChimp, think about what angle you will take. Ultimately, the newsletter should offer value and not serve as a weekly showcase of what you and your business have been up to. Some self-promotion should always be injected, but strive for a balance. Also, consider ways to cut down on the time it takes to assemble and write your newsletter. This will play into your design strategy (e.g. highly templated) and overall approach to curating content. The examples that follow reflect two ways of doing this on a limited (time) budget:

WHO CAN I COPY?

Forerunner Ventures (forerunnerventures.com) puts out a really great newsletter every Saturday morning. Since the company focuses on retail startups, the digest is a rundown of the top retail news of the week, along with some updates from their portfolio companies. While the content mostly links out to full-length articles, the true value of the newsletter lies in its curation and summaries, which oftentimes replace the need to read the full articles.

If you're regularly producing content that's hosted on your own blog, or other blogs, a simple weekly digest is a great way to promote your thought leadership without having to reinvent the wheel. See our digest below, which simply compiles or top news and blog pieces (blog.and.co) each week.

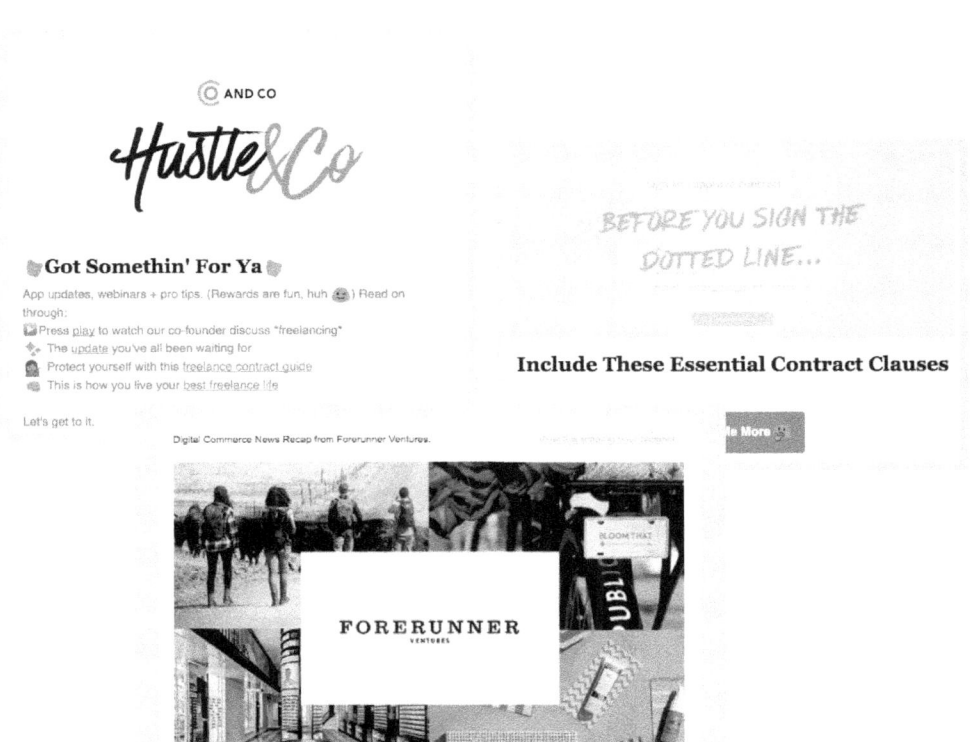

Hacking Independence

THE ORACLE HACK

Look ahead to keep your business booming now & in the future.

WHAT IS IT?
When you're in the day-to-day grind of running your freelance business, it can be easy to lose sight of the big picture—that is, where your business is going, where the industry is headed, and which opportunities might present themselves in the future. Being an "oracle" in this sense is less about predicting the future and more about following trends that unlock opportunities for you in the months, quarters and years ahead.

HOW DO I DO IT?
The Oracle Hack can be as easy as setting a quarterly calendar reminder for yourself to write down some of the trends you're seeing in the marketplace. Has there been an uptick in a specific ask from clients? Is there less demand for certain capabilities as there used to be? Are there external forces at play (e.g. emerging platforms or design techniques) that are relatively new and still developing? Spend a couple of hours each quarter jotting down your observations, and then consider how you might test your hypotheses iteratively with minimum investment.

WHO CAN I COPY?
If you're reading this in 2017, you know that Amazon just bought Whole Foods. But why would an online retail giant want to own a brick

and mortar grocery chain? Amazon knows that it's only a matter of time until the grocery delivery system becomes commonplace, and before then, they'll be providing discounts to Whole Foods customers by using your Amazon Prime account.

Consider Tesla Motors, which struggled in its early days, and almost went under several times. But Elon Musk knew that electric cars were inevitable, so he put everything he had behind the idea, and now owns the world's most valuable car company only 15 years later. The greatest business leaders look to the future when making their biggest plays, and you can do.

In fact, there are much smaller and medium sized bets that anyone can make. Find resources that help you understand how markets are shifting, and make sure you're a part of those markets when they evolve. LinkedIn, AngelList, Glassdoor, and Google Trends are just a few examples of tools you can use to get ahead of the curve.

THE OVERACHIEVER HACK

Overdeliver on expectations to increase your recurring revenue.

Contributed by Kat Boogaard, freelance writer (katboogaard.com)

WHAT IS IT?
Any employer appreciates someone who goes above and beyond the call of duty, and the same holds true for freelance clients. Meeting expectations is crucial, but exceeding them is even better. Not only does going the extra mile demonstrate to your clients the exceptional value that you offer them, but it also fosters an even better relationship—which can lead to even more work and a longer engagement. Long story short: Don't skate by on the bare minimum. The extra work is well worth the investment.

HOW DO I DO IT?
Always think of ways that you can surpass expectations. Perhaps that's as simple as beating a deadline. Maybe it's stepping up when that client is in a pinch with a last-minute project. Or, it could even involve an extra piece of work—think a custom GIF to bring clarity to your article, for example—that adds even more value to your submission.

WHO CAN I COPY?

Ask yourself these questions to provide excellent client service:

- Have I followed the client's specifications for the project?
- Have I communicated regularly throughout the course of the assignment?
- Have I delivered the finished project by the deadline (or earlier)?
- Have I added something above and beyond what was requested?
- Have I asked the client for feedback?

THE PODCAST HACK

Pitch yourself as a guest expert on business podcasts.

WHAT IS IT?
Who says radio is dead? Podcasting is big business and you don't have to start your own show and build your own audience to reap the benefits. There are hundreds of podcasts out there currently that cover a range of niche topics that may or may not be relevant to you and your business. Given the frequency of shows, podcast programmers and hosts are always looking for smart guests to contribute to the conversation.

HOW DO I DO IT?
Create a list of podcasts with decently-sized followings that are relevant to your business. Relevance is key, since you want to make sure your time is being used wisely and your involvement will get you in front of potential prospects or collaborators.

First, search the iTunes store (itunes.apple.com/us/genre/podcasts) or podcast-specific engines like Listen Notes (listennotes.com) to discover programs that are relevant to your interests. Maintain a list of these shows and keep it regularly updated. Visit the websites for each podcast to pitch yourself to the show, succinctly explaining why you'd make a great guest. Bullet out short phrases that give the host a quick but high-level overview as to which topics you're able to discuss.

WHO CAN I COPY?

Want to learn more? Follow this comprehensive primer from author and business speaker Heidi Thorne: podcastmotor.com/getting-on-podcasts-as-a-guest.

Hacking Independence

THE PRODUCT IS KING (PIK) HACK

Having a slick website is great, but your work needs to live up to the promise.

WHAT IS IT?
You can have the best marketing and most exceptional client service in the world, but if your product isn't living up to the hype, then you will never see your business truly flourish. The Product Is King Hack is as intuitive as it sounds, and it means retaining an ongoing and borderline obsessive focus on the excellence of the product you're delivering the clients. Whether that's consultative guidance or a tangible deliverable (e.g. a design asset or product), remember that—at day's end—the most important aspect of your business is the product.

HOW DO I DO IT?
So, with all of the various tasks that come with running your own business, from paying bills to tax prep and everything in between, how can you ensure your product is consistently exceeding expectations and evolving over time, in accordance with customer needs and market trends? Here are some thought-starters:

- **Get feedback:** Be open to critique and suggestions when it comes to your product and how you're delivering it to partners. Ask partners, friends, and trusted peers to weigh in (and not just once!). Iterative and ongoing feedback will allow you to optimize over time, consistently improving as part of your overall process.

Hacking Independence

- **Steal from others:** Okay, so we don't mean actual stealing, but as the saying goes, "Talent imitates and genius steals." Become a student of your industry. Follow peers in your space (including competitors), taking note of what others are doing that might work for you. Be open to remixing other people's approaches, thereby making them your own.
- **Schedule quarterly check-ins:** For most freelancers, life can get so busy that it's hard to make time for projects outside of the realm of billable work. However, assessing and optimizing your product on a regular basis is mission critical to the future growth of your business. Lock a half day in your schedule once a quarter to review feedback and score yourself against what's working and what can be improved. End each session with a list of actionable bullets for what to test, or change entirely, in the months ahead.

WHO CAN I COPY?
Mimic these product-first companies in your own career:

- Volkswagen Group, known for product excellence in the auto industry.
- Amazon, which rose to prominence without any splashy branding or PR efforts.
- Apple, especially during the Steve Jobs years.
- Ferragamo, which is known for making quality goods that last a lifetime.

THE PUBLIC INFORMATION HACK

Scrape publicly available data to surface leads. It's free prospecting.

WHAT IS IT?
Each year, business owners spend millions of dollars paying money to acquire "lists" of prospective clients. These lists are often collected in seedy ways and do not deliver the freshest list of potential leads for your money. Fortunately, there's a treasure trove of publicly available data to help you build your own lists–and with a bit of elbow grease, you can save money and build a powerful CRM database for your sales outreach.

HOW DO I DO IT?
First, know your customer, and understand what types of public filings they might create in their personal and business lives. Filings like LLCs, S Corps, Corporations, DBAs, and more are public record, and these are just a few of the many public filings that can be accessed by anyone. Most of these documents are recorded at the county level, and can be discovered by going to your county clerk or county websites. Some counties will even provide a CD of certain items for a fee.

WHO CAN I COPY?
Almost every county will have a different system for housing their public records, so each case is unique in how to approach their system,

but a simple online search will help you find the website or office where these records are held. For example, for business records, you can search "Fictitious Business Name Search" and the county you're interested in. Here is an example of Los Angeles County's website for Business Name Records: apps1.lavote.net/CLERK/FBN_Search.cfm.

Hacking Independence

THE RETARGETING HACK

Steal a page from all of those websites that are straight up stalking you.

WHAT IS IT?
Ever notice an ad that's, for lack of better words, following you around the internet? Chances are, it's a shirt you abandoned in a shopping cart after you realized you probably should be saving your money. Or perhaps it's that Airbnb property you were scoping before you got distracted by one of 27 browser tabs you have open. How do they do it? How do they know?

It's pretty simple, actually. Marketers place pixels on their websites, which are basically just lines of code that track various analytics. When you visit a site, it registers your identity as a "cookie," or unique (and don't worry, anonymized) identifier that tells the marketer you have been on the site, and even on that specific page. Once your cookie is registered, that data can be used to serve you ads in the future, all across the internet via various ad networks and exchanges. Crazy, right? It's big business for marketers and a bread-and-butter strategy for many brands.

HOW DO I DO IT?
Adroll, Steelhouse, Google Retargeting, Facebook Retargeting and Perfect Audience are good places to begin vetting for the right partner.

Hacking Independence

Most of these platforms do not require a minimum spend, although you will need enough website traffic coming into warrant a campaign. If you do not yet have sizable traffic to your site, this hack might be one to revisit later on.

WHO CAN I COPY?
Sometimes, media campaigns like retargeting and Google Adwords can be used in out of the box, albeit cost-effective, ways. Consider the case of of a young Y&R creative, Alec Brownstein, who ran an Adwords campaign, which is based on targeting specific keywords, against the names of prominent agency creative directors. Based on the insights that CDs will often Google their own names to find instances of their work on the web, he ran targeted ads against a list, in which he inquired about job opportunities in the copy.

Web ⊞ Show options...

Hey, Ian Reichenthal
www.alecbrownstein.com   Gooogling yourself is a lot of fun. Hiring me is fun, too.

The brilliant campaign worked, and on a limited budget, he landed his dream job.

Hacking Independence

THE SASSY SUBJECT LINE HACK

Get people to actually open your cold emails.

WHAT IS IT?
More than 2 million emails are sent every second. Most of these, are of course unsolicited promotions from stores you bought one product from five years ago, or perhaps impassioned outreach from Nigerian princes. As a freelancer, you know that email is one of the best ways to get in touch with potential partners—but how the heck are you supposed to stand out? It all starts with the subject line.

HOW DO I DO IT?
As the adage goes, you've only got one chance to make a first impression. How are you going to get someone who doesn't recognize your name or email to hit open? There are a few approaches you might take, outlined below:

- **The narcissistic angle:** Try putting their name front and center in the subject: "Maria: Coffee next week?"
- **The super direct angle:** Say what you plan to do for the potential customer, e.g. "How about some new copy that converts?"
- **The shock-and-awe:** Are you the kind of person to chuck up a Hail Mary and hope for the best? Perhaps you've tried this person a few times, but nothing has worked. Write something weird, but not too weird, e.g. "Oh my god, who let all these pandas out of the zoo?"

WHO CAN I COPY?

There are a number of blog posts online that share subject lines most likely to get an open. While these are mostly targeted at mass email marketing strategies, you can still borrow some best practices in your one-to-one outreach.

Here are a few that come up often:

- Hey
- Sorry
- Oops
- Thanks
- Don't open this
- Gift for you
- Meet your next [insert role here]
- [###] ideas for your business (fill in with actual number)
- Quick favor?

Some other tips:

- Most people now open emails in mobile. Keep headlines short!
- A study from Experian found that emojis increased open rates by 45 percent
- Tie the subject line to your opening sentence. E.g. if you use "Sorry," follow it up with "I know I've sent you a few of these, but I think I could really help with [XYZ]."

THE SEO CONTENT HACK

Publish content that can help you get discovered.

Contributed by Maddy Osman, SEO Content Strategist (the-blogsmith.com)

WHAT IS IT?
The one piece of content marketing every freelancer should engage in is blogging. Try not to think of it as extra work that you don't get paid for, as it's truly an easy way to organically bring in relevant customers from search. The right blog content can effectively convert a visitor into a customer. The key is to make sure that you're not just blogging for the sake of it, but blogging with a purpose. You can use your blog to connect with your target audience via search through the use of appropriate keywords.

HOW DO I DO IT?
Climb to the top of organic search rankings and watch your traffic soar.

There are a number of keyword tools out there, but the tried and true (and free!) gold standard is Google's Keyword Planner. Though it's technically an Adwords tool, it can give a lot of insight regarding search volume and the level of competition for a given keyword.

So, throw in a keyword on Google Keyword Planner and see what suggestions it gives you. Higher search volume is not always better, (we're aiming for quality, not quantity here), but anything over 1,000 searches per month is probably worth trying to rank for. Low-medium competition is best—a new website or someone just starting out with SEO will not be able to compete with high competition keywords.

Fancy tools like Moz or SEMrush can give you more granular data, but they can get expensive on a freelancer's budget. So, take what you can from Google Keyword Planner to get started on your SEO content mission.

Refine your keyword based on the suggestions from Google Keyword Planner until you've found the perfect fit. Don't forget to factor in intent—What does the keyword say about your customer's stage in the buying process? It's important to create content to grab attention, to assist with consideration, and finally, to close the deal.

Of course, once you've found the ideal keyword, the key to success is proper onsite SEO implementation. If your website makes use of WordPress, figuring this out is as simple as installing the Yoast plugin.

WHO CAN I COPY?
Andy Crestodina (orbitmedia.com/team/andy-crestodina) of Orbit Media Studios implements and shares his SEO content strategy best practices.

THE SOCIAL PROOF HACK

Lean on the reputation and brand cache of others to boost your own cred.

WHAT IS IT?
Social proof is a psychological incidence in which people look to surrounding cues to navigate a new or unfamiliar situation. In the context of your self-managed business, social proof means giving prospective customers powerful cues that indicate you have experience, credibility and influence.

HOW DO I DO IT?
In a personal branding sense, social proof can come to life in a variety of ways. Here are a few to start:

- Leverage client logos on your portfolio page. Lead with your biggest brand name clients, even if your partnership with them is limited in scope. As a general rule of them, it's best to ask for forgiveness rather than permission when it comes to using your partners' logos on your marketing materials. That said, use your discretion: you know your clients better than anyone.
- Use social share counts (Facebook, Twitter, LinkedIn) on your blog if you have the traffic to back it up. If you don't have the numbers, wait until you do. Negative social proof is far worse than none at all.

- Ask for testimonials. Place these on your LinkedIn and portfolio, and use them in outreach emails as needed. See "The Word-of-Mouth Hack" for how to ask for these.

WHO CAN I COPY?

For example Kristi Hines (kristihines.com) and Sarah Chang (sarahlichang.com):

THE SIGNATURE HACK

Max out the marketing real estate of your email signature.

WHAT IS IT?
Your email signature is more than just a formality; it's prime real estate for marketing. Use the opportunity to reinforce your credibility and promote your services every single time you hit "send."

HOW DO I DO IT?
Step back and think about what you want to reinforce in your signature, beyond your name, title and contact information. Perhaps you want to promote the e-book you just authored, or maybe you want to share a link to your latest Medium byline. List out your top 3 "things" to promote, keeping in mind that you might need to make cuts.

A simple Google search will yield hundreds if not thousands of templates you can use for inspiration. HubSpot also has a great guide that provides simple pro-tips that will ensure a clean and readable design.

Hacking Independence

WHO CAN I COPY?

Here are some examples to reference as you craft your own.

   *Get personal by adding your photo.*

Hype your portfolios.

  *Make it pop with an animated GIF.*

Promote content with a clickable banner.

77

Hacking Independence

THE SOMETHING FOR NOTHING HACK

Because everyone loves a freebie. And freebies can lead to money.

Contributed by Jacob Cass, Graphic Designer (justcreative.com)

WHAT IS IT?
Everyone loves something for free and other blogs love sharing freebies, especially in roundup compilation posts, so offer something valuable for free and the links will come in. To put this into perspective, for the past few years I've offered a free logo design inspiration e-book, in exchange for an email address. This has not only garnered thousands of email subscribers, but it has been featured on many free e-book compilation posts, giving links back to my website, further strengthening my search rankings.

HOW DO I DO IT?
Consider what unique service or skill you're willing to invest some time into for the sake of new business. Remember that these hours will be non-billable, but with the right approach and distribution strategy, it will serve as a formidable pipeline for new business down the road. If it's a piece of content you're offering, you might want to enlist design help or use a sleek template to bring your words to life. You can set up

Hacking Independence

a simple landing page with a service like MailChimp or Squarespace, or build it into your blog or website, as I've done below.

WHO CAN I COPY?

Check out my logo design e-book at justcreative.com.

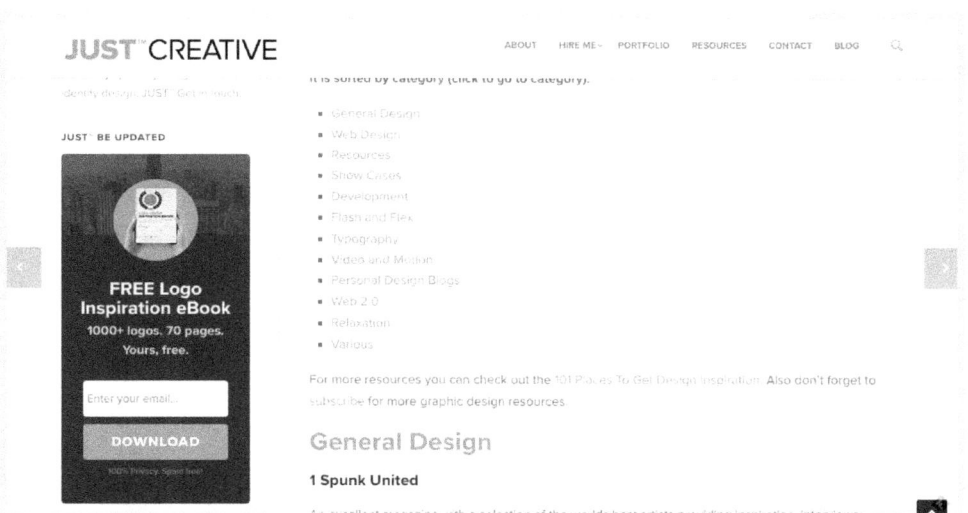

THE STRATEGIC PARTNER HACK

Make freelancing a team sport by collaborating where it makes sense.

WHAT IS IT?
"Strategic partnerships" is a core function at many businesses, and just because you're a team of one doesn't mean you shouldn't reap the benefits of building a network of collaborators. For example, a freelance engineer working with startups might team up with a UX designer targeting the same industry so that you can refer projects and clients to each other where it makes sense. Partnerships are also great for co-marketing efforts (this book is a prime example!), allowing you to divvy up the work and conquer two audiences for the "price" of one.

HOW DO I DO IT?
From a business development standpoint, think about complementary functions that do not compete with your own offering. Some pairings that make sense include:

- Sales specialists and marketing/comms strategists
- Event managers and PR specialists
- PR specialists and content marketers
- Content marketers and growth hackers
- Content marketers and designers
- Designers and engineers
- Engineers and product managers

Hacking Independence

For co-marketing, the nature of partnerships will depend upon your audience. Think about which types of non-competitive businesses or professionals are vying to reach a similar audience. Prior to approaching a prospective partner, put some thinking into the value exchange for both you/your business and them. You should be able to clearly articulate the benefit to them before beginning the conversation.

WHO CAN I COPY?

Here are some examples of successful co-marketing:

Uber and Spotify: A match made in heaven, this co-branding effort allows Uber riders to set the soundtrack to their ride from within the Uber app.

Lyft and Taco Bell: Not to be outdone, Lyft has partnered with Lyft for "Taco Mode," making late-night snacking more seamless than ever.

 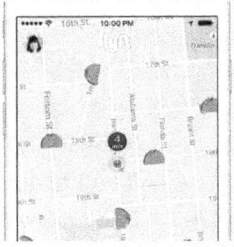

Sketch and Invision: A leader in content marketing, Invision recently launched a book in partnership with Sketch. Claim your copy at: invisionapp.com/ ecourses/design-with-invision- craft-and-sketch.

81

THE USER RESEARCH HACK

Really get to know what makes your customers tick.

Contributed by Format (www.format.com).

WHAT IS IT?
When you're building your business, you can't rely on metrics alone. You need to talk to your customers and make sure you understand their problems. At Format, our user researchers conduct phone interviews and in-person meetings to gather qualitative information. They want to know why customers create online portfolios using Format, and how Format can continue developing products that those customers actually need.

HOW DO I DO IT?
If you're not talking to your customers, you need to start reaching out immediately. It doesn't matter what size or stage your business is, your customers will help you grow in the right direction. Even if you're a freelancer with a couple of clients, call them up and ask open-ended questions like:

- Why did you need to hire someone with my skills?
- How did you find out about my company?
- When you refer my business to another client, what words do you use to describe me?

After speaking to a few customers, you'll start to see trends. Do they use language like "reliable and quick" or do they say "informed and professional"? This gives a big indication of your strengths, the problems you're solving for customers and how you should be marketing your business.

WHO CAN I COPY?
The first thing you should do is read about Bob Moesta's concept "Jobs to be Done" (hbr.org/2016/09/know-your-customers-jobs-to-be-done). It's a framework for user research that we use at Format. The overall theory is that your business doesn't just provide a product or service, it provides a solution for a job your customer needs to "be done."

You need to speak to your users to figure out the "jobs to be done", a process that involves more emotional and psychological probing than dry interrogation. There's a good beginner script on JTBD.info (jtbd.info/a-script-to-kickstart-your-jobs-to-be-done-interviews-2768164761d7) with interview questions you should ask. It's a start in the right direction, then you can adapt the script to suit you and your business.

Hacking Independence

THE VIP HACK

Have a "you can't sit with us" mentality, without being a total jerk.

Contributed by Ashley Nowicki, Founder, AUCTOR (latinforpioneer.io)

WHAT IS IT?
As an entrepreneur running your own business, time is money. And sometimes the most value you can bring to the business is protecting your time. Pay close attention to who you spend your time with, and how you spend it.

HOW DO I DO IT?
Don't take on the highest paying client if you don't believe in the work. Save money so you can stay afloat even if the types of projects that excite you dry up for a bit. Avoid taking on projects that don't challenge you in a new, yet terrifying, way. Don't go to the party if you don't think you will actually walk away with an interesting new contact or possible lead. Say "no" to a couple of those, "Can we grab coffee?" favors your friends and previous colleagues ask you to do that don't really provide you with any benefit. Respect your time. Respect your energy. Respect your bandwidth. And your business will feel the immediate impact.

Hacking Independence

WHO CAN I COPY?

Tim Ferriss' "The 4-Hour Workweek" clearly articulates these principles in an easy-to-follow format. Don't have time to read the whole thing? Check out a summary at wikisummaries.org/wiki/The_4-Hour_Workweek, or browse the visual recap below.

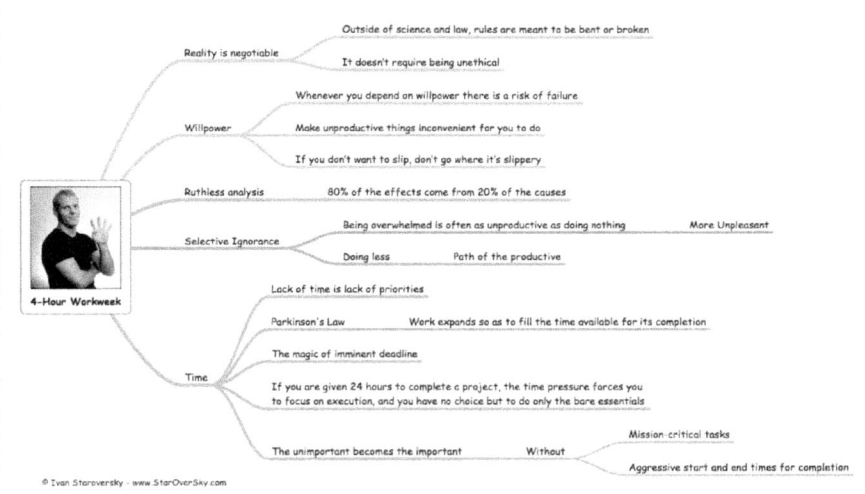

Hacking Independence

THE WORD-OF-MOUTH HACK

What other people say about you is more powerful than what you say about yourself.

WHAT IS IT?
Per AND CO's recent Slash Workers study (and.co/slash-workers), 91 percent of independent workers said they typically find new clients via word-of-mouth referrals—far and away the largest driver of new business across all tactics. Great work begets referrals, but there are ways to increase the volume and quality of your testimonials. The big secret: Just ask!

HOW TO DO IT?
When you approach a client, first and foremost, be gracious of their time. It's also important to cherry pick your best clients only. These are the projects that you felt the most "on" during, or long-term partners you trust. In your note, describe why referrals are important, why you chose to reach out to them and what, in particular, you are looking for in their writeup. Help them help you!

WHO CAN I COPY?
Steal this template:

Hey, [NAME]:

I've really enjoyed working with you on project [X] for [GENUINE REASON]. As you likely know, having testimonials is important to my business and I'm curious if you'd be open to sharing your experience with me for use on [WEBSITE/LINKEDIN/WHEREVER].

I know you have a packed schedule, but would you be open to providing two to three sentences on [SPECIFICALLY STATE WHAT YOU WANT THEM TO SHARE, E.G. "My ability to work in Sketch"]?

Thank you,
[NAME]

Hacking Independence

THE WORK-YOUR-WORKSPACE HACK

Use your coffee shop or coworking space for the networking opportunity it is.

WHAT IS IT?
Many independents work remotely from coworking spaces, coffee shops and other communal areas. In these environments, it can be easy to be insular, shrouding ourselves from others with big headphones and the like. While focus is a great attribute, remember that your impromptu office space could be where you find your next client or collaborator.

HOW TO DO IT?
Networking in shared office spaces can be as easy as attending that once-a-month happy hour, or striking up conversation with your desk mate over coffee. More formally, many communities have Facebook groups and other ways for connecting and building your business. Another pro-tip: Go analog by creating a simple printed flier that you can place strategically in a high-traffic area. State who you are, what kind of partners you take on and provide the relevant information needed for people to reach out.

WHO CAN I COPY?

Here are some thought-starters from successful workspace networkers:

- Does your coworking space host panels or lunch and learns? **Offer yourself up as an expert in your field, providing some free insights for your fellow co-workers.**
- **Utilize message boards, Slack channels and email listservs** to offer up your services where they make sense. Be sure your participation in these are not self-serving and transactional. Establish yourself as a trusted member of the community before going in for the hard sell.
- **Be present.** Even if you pay for an office, find windows to be present in common spaces—even if that just means taking time to grab a coffee or eat lunch out in the open. Avail yourself to social opportunities throughout the day to broaden your network.
- Many coworking spaces will host monthly or quarterly socials or happy hours. **Take time to make an appearance at these events to broaden your network.**

CONCLUSION

"Big thoughts are fun to romanticize, but it's many small insights coming together that bring big ideas into the world."

– Scott Berken, author, "The Myths of Innovation"

As a freelancer, you might feel as though it's you against the world. In many ways, it is. This is the great challenge and great opportunity that comes with the independent work lifestyle. You're dictating your own course, but you're also responsible for making all of the things happen, big and small, to drive your career forward. And, as the adage goes, little things make big things happen.

Any successful entrepreneur that big changes don't happen all at once. In fact, progress is most successfully achieved by through the implementation of small, measurable changes that can be optimized or improved upon over time. We hope this book provided some hacks that you can begin using immediately, and we'd love to hear your feedback at hello@andco.nyc or on Twitter twitter.com/andco.

Want even more tools to help grow your business and make your life easier? Check out:

- **The Gig List:** A curated weekly newsletter featuring the top ten freelance and remote work gigs we could dig up, served with a dose of sarcasm for your reading pleasure: and.co/gig-list
- **Williams&Harricks:** A physical demand letter generator for late-paying clients. and.co/williams-harricks
- **The Standard Freelance Contract:** Never waste time mocking up a service agreement again. We teamed up with Freelancers Union to help you customize and download your own agreement in minutes: and.co/the-freelance-contract
- **Freelance Task Manager:** A virtual assistant for helping you tackle the things that need to get done right now? Yes please. Sign up for AND CO for free and starting using our smart project organizer today. Start at and.co
- **Welcome to Your Independence:** New to the freelance game? Add this to your reading list: and.co/how-to-freelance
- **ANYWHERE:** With the digital nomad movement on the rise, we consulted dozens of successful nomads to uncover what you need to know before taking the leap. Download the free book at and.co/digital-nomad-book

Thanks to our contributors:
The about.me Team, Kat Boogaard, The Format Team, Jacob Cass, Kaleigh Moore & Creative Class, Ashley Nowicki & AUCTOR, Maddy Osman, Max Pete, Dennis Williams II, Charles Shapard, Andrew Yang & 500px

Editors:
Katie Perry, Martin Strutz

Layout/Illustration:
Martin Strutz/Basia Grzybowska

Created and published by AND CO Ventures Inc.
©Copyright 2017. All rights reserved.

www.ingramcontent.com/pod-product-compliance
Lightning Source LLC
Chambersburg PA
CBHW050232230526
45470CB00005B/1916